Becoming Sassily Me: Acknowledging and Regaining Lost Confidence and Power

Tammie T. Polk

Photo by JD Mason on Unsplash

ISBN: 9798666276396

DEDICATION

To anyone who has decided that enough
is truly enough...

To anyone who feels like they no longer
know who they are...

This is for you!

CONTENTS

Becoming Sassily Me: Acknowledging and Regaining
Lost Confidence and Power

ACKNOWLEDGMENTS

To my Lord and Savior Jesus Christ...
To Tomica Shavers, whose support
pushed me to finish this book in merely
hours...
To my readers, who still smile and shake
their heads when they hear I have
something new out...
To my family, who knows that I write to
help...
To my mentors, who laugh, yet never
give up on me...
To my inner circle, who can only say that
this is why they love me LOL...

I truly am trying to help save the world
by the power of the blank page and I
couldn't do it without you!

CONCERN: AM I LOSING MY CONFIDENCE AND POWER?

Think about it…

It starts small…

Downplaying your talents…

Not saying no when you know you need to…

Allowing people's opinions to matter more than they should…

Making excuses and rationalizing why they're right about you…

You've been made to feel guilty because you were powerful and confident. The sad part is that you ran head-on into someone who had a problem with that. They know that what they see in you is special and that you're meant to do something awesome in this world. Yet, because of who they are, you listen to them.

This can be your best friend, a co-worker, a family member—anyone. You find yourself slowly fading into the background and, at first, you're okay with it because some of the pressure that you've been feeling is now gone.

You dismiss the anger that's rising inside of you because things that used to matter to you are resurfacing and you're confused.

You attribute the fact that you're less vocal to wanting a break from the demands that once weighed you down. You start to wonder if those demands were weighing you down or if someone made you think that they were.

You stop doing things that you were known to do, enjoyed doing, and even made money from. From there, you notice that everyone around you is healthy, happy, and thriving, never admitting that you're struggling.

When you finally decide to give energy to truly looking at yourself in the mirror, you ask yourself this question: Am I losing my confidence and power?

The short answer is yes! Because that one person came to you or because that one bad experience looms over you, you have started to think that what was once rare and precious about you no longer exists.

You look around and notice that you aren't dressing the same. You went from being bright and cheerful in your dress to throwing on the first decent thing you see.

You fix yourself up just enough to not get talked about, knowing that you were never like that before. Your physical appearance is merely a formality.

You stop eating healthy as you used to, trading practicality for nutrition. Some days, you won't eat at all.

What does this have to do with losing confidence and power? More than you think...

Part of Becoming Sassily You in this area is asking yourself a very important question: Am I taking care of myself and what do I need to do to make myself a priority again.

When you start losing confidence and power, you will dismiss this question because you don't want to answer it.

Answering the questions is going to force you to admit that the answer is no and that you've let yourself go in more ways than you ever thought possible.

The key to regaining your lost power here is to look at what you've been reading, watching, listening to, and doing along with who you've been hanging around. Is it time for you to start weeding people, places, and things out of your life?

Do you care that things with you are out of whack? If the answer to that question is no and you say so without hesitation, then stop reading now because nothing else penned here will help you.

But, if you're ready to do something about what's going on with you because you KNOW that you're off and need to get back on track, then let's name the work is and commit to doing said work.

Naming the work means looking back at the things mentioned at the beginning of this chapter.

First, there is downplaying your talents. When you are losing your confidence and power, one of the first problems you have is that you begin to think that you are unworthy of any compliments or accolades. Now, this is different from humility and meekness and I'll tell you how.

With humility and meekness, you acknowledge that you are talented; however, you don't want people falling over themselves about it. You want to do, let it help who it will help, and keep going. You can slide confidence right on in with these two!

When confidence and power are waning, you will start saying things like,

"Why do they keep telling me that's good...it's not all that special! Why are they making such a big deal out of nothing?" You won't understand why they are trying to get you to see that it is as good as it is.

Not only that, but you will also find that you will become angered by anyone who says that you were never like this before. You will remember that you tooted your own horn the regular without being obnoxious or facetious with it and will wonder where that part of you went!

You'll remember being that way and how it made you feel, yet you will think that there's no possible way for you to be that person again, angering you even more. You find yourself near tears or in full out ugly cry mode because you can't believe you got to that point....let's move on because I don't want you to get stuck here for too long!

Second, there is not saying no when you know you need to. I am certain that I don't have to tell you about how this leads to an extreme level of burnout.

When you are losing your confidence and power, you will allow people to make you feel guilty for having something else to do. You will start to tell yourself that what you have going on can wait, be moved, or even canceled so that you can do what you're being asked to do.

In the past, you would have stood your ground, but over time, you've allowed people to wear you down and, no matter how pissed off you REALLY are, you do what they need to have done so that you can get them out of your face. The problem with that is there is nothing left for you and what you need to do.

You'll tell yourself that it's okay that you didn't get your stuff done, yet you'll become agitated because your to-do list lengthens every time you blink. Then, when you do stand up and say that you need time to do some of those important things, they will hit you with, "I know I ask you to do a lot and I really do appreciate you. Just do me this one last favor right quick and I'll leave you alone." You know it's not true, yet you do it anyway.

Next thing you know, they ask for something else... then something else... then one more thing and they're done... then one last thing and they're done... then "I promise I won't ask you to do anything else after this." Now, the time you thought you had is gone and you're having dinner with doubt, talking about how you will never get back on track.

Because you are now without confidence in yourself and powerless, you start to lash out and they turn it right back around on you because they don't want to own their role in how you're feeling. They say that you could have said no, you'll tell them that you did, and they will find some way to still make you responsible for how things went. From there, you're done talking because you realize they will never acknowledge that they're wrong.

Now you have no clue how to get the feeling off you, which leads to our third piece of work to do.

Allowing people's opinions to matter more than they should is the result of the third piece of work. Although you know they are wrong, you will allow yourself to wonder if you need to do more to make time for other people. You will say that your lashing out came from a place of selfishness and that is NOT the case!

You will go right back to doing things for them because you don't want them to think ill of you and that kind of motivation is unhealthy for everyone involved in the situation. Your confidence and power are now being replaced with unnecessary, self-inflicted fear and angst that will not be easy to overcome.

They have you right where they want you. They know that all they have to do is act like they are mad at you for taking time to yourself and you'll come running. They'll feel bad for doing it, yet you'll never know it and they'll mask it because they're getting what they want. They will say something about it afterward, but they will make sure that you NEVER know they said it. If you find out they said it, they will deny it and now you're public enemy number one over something you weren't even privy to happening!

Be careful in how you react to this because it can worsen in the blink of an eye! While you know it has nothing to do with you, if you allow them to throw you into the rabbit hole, you will come out seeing yourself as the problem, which leads to our final piece of work.

Making excuses and rationalizing why they're right about you is what they want you to do. You may think that doesn't make sense, yet it does. Because they see where you can go and what you can do when you have that confidence and power they are stripping away from you, they want to make you believe that you are doing things wrong. This will force you to start making unnecessary changes and the only ones who will be happy about these changes are them!

When you are losing your confidence and power, you will come up with every reason that they are right about why you need to dial your life back. How so? Think about this...

They will attack the way that you dress, especially if you wear a lot of bright colors and patterns. You know that you're wearing colors, styles, and patterns that match your body type as well as your personality, yet they will attack you into wearing mute colors with no shape and no life. You won't see that, though. All you will see is that they are upset because you're "making them look bad", "drawing too much attention to yourself," or the fact that they are always complaining about how you dress. The key here is to think about what they're saying, but don't take it at face value because there may not be anything wrong with how you dress at all!

They will attach your personality. Before now, they loved everything about you, yet as you began to grow in who you are and outgrow them, now you're too outspoken, talk too loud, think too much of yourself, or are always showing off. This usually happens when they have problems in their own lives that they refuse to make better. Instead of working on what's going on with them, they seek to bring the same problems into your life, making you miserable. That's not what you'll see...

You'll start to replay conversations they

were involved in and will take their reactions as bad things when, in reality, there was nothing wrong with what you said or did! Now you're battling with confusion because you don't get what's wrong with what you did or said and, because of who they are in your life, you will start holding your tongue.

The problem with this one is that you will become a mute chameleon if you're not careful! The key here is to know the difference between what they're saying and what is actually happening. If they are right, know that you can still be you and dial it back. If they aren't, be brave enough to respectfully check them and keep being you!

They will attack what you do for a living., especially if you are in a field that they tried before, and it didn't go well for them. You are thriving in it and they can't stand it, so they will bring every negative scenario they can think of into your mind and will have you quitting your job or closing your business out of fear and doubt! Because of who they are to you, you will tell yourself that they would know because they were at it for longer than you have been and that your success in that field was merely a fluke and won't last as long as you thought it would.

You are risking your livelihood to appease the self-inflicted life dissatisfaction of someone else! Destroying your life for someone who you know is not going to help you because they can't help you is NOT what you want to do. Plus, if you DO end up doing what they ask and they do offer their help, it's going to be in a field that is going to drain everything you have left out of you! You will end up feeling much worse...

They will attack who you hang around, especially if you have an inner circle that they envy. Because they are always alone, they will plant seeds of doubt in you that will have you scrutinizing the people who inspire, challenge, support, and motivate you FOR NO REASON! They have given you NO reason to think what this person is trying to make you believe, yet you will give energy to what they say.

The question you have is to ask yourself is if the relationship with the person with the problem is worth the relationship with your inner circle. As the saying goes, "Blood isn't always family." With that in mind, you need to be careful because you will end up losing someone you can't afford to lose! They will see what this person is trying to do and will warn you against them, yet you will side with the other person, potentially permanently damaging your relationship.

When you lose someone in your inner circle, getting them back will be close to impossible! Don't break your own heart to appease someone who is going to continue to be the way they are while YOU are the one making all the changes!

Now, I want you to grab your journal and answer the questions that are there. Once you're done, you will have the change to free write about how you feel.

CONFESSION: OKAY, I LOST MY CONFIDENCE AND POWER!

Piggybacking off the last chapter, we are now at the point where you realize that everything, or even a few things, that I mentioned is actually happening in your life.

You realize that your confidence and power are gone!

Another part of Becoming Sassily You is learning to deal with the emotions that arise from this happening...

First, the anger and frustration you feel

are warranted. I know that you're kicking yourself for letting it get to this point. Instead of beating yourself up and down, process that anger and frustration. Ask yourself what was the last straw that made you start making the changes in each situation.

Second, the guilt is something you need to handle before it gets the best of you. Focusing on what happened that got you to this point will drive you MAD, causing you to not deal with anything and now you are just as miserable as the person who goaded you into making the changes. One tough thing I will challenge you to do here is to have a conversation with the person and ask them WHY they wanted you to make the changes. In so doing, be prepared for this to be put on overdrive!

They will see the changes that you made

and that they were wrong for you, yet they may choose to eat fire before they admit that they were wrong in making you feel as guilty as you do. You may have to ask those hard questions and force them to admit what they were really doing to you, which won't be easy! Be prepared for them to not want to deal with this EVER, no matter what you do. Sometimes, people will only seek closure on their terms, so you can't allow yourself to continue to feel guilty. It's time to make your plan to move forward!

Third, you must process that someone close to you may no longer be in your life. I bring this up now because it is something that is a result of the other two. When you have lost your confidence and power, your inner circle will notice! The problem is what we mentioned in the last chapter—you can't get them back and it's killing you!

You're angry, frustrated, and feeling guilty because this person is now out of your life. You're fighting back tears and that heated feeling in your body because you remember what that person was to you...and you miss that with them. You're missing the awesome things going on in their lives that you know you would have been a part of had you not listened to this other person.

Finally, you must deal with the fact that you've turned your life on its head for no good reason. The key here is looking at the exact things that you gave up, changed, and shifted and own it! Will this produce anger, frustration, and guilt? Yes, it will; however, you can't let that keep you from doing something about it.

I'm making this chapter short and sweet because I want to give you the chance to write out how you're feeling and process the things we talked about here. You'll need a clear head for the next chapter because it's going to sting!

COMPREHENSION: THIS HAPPENED BECAUSE I LOST MY CONFIDENCE AND POWER!

In this chapter, I want to talk about seven things that you've lost by trading your confidence and power for someone else's vision of what your life should be. When it comes to Becoming Sassily You, these seven things are going to have to be set back aright and quickly before more damage is done.

If you know my work in any way, these are going to sound VERY familiar...

You've lost MONEY! Making the changes that they asked you to make has put you in a financial bind that they don't understand and won't help you rectify. You've shifted so much that even your bank account is wondering what is wrong with you. At this point, you're picking up the pieces before you lose everything you have. As you wipe away the tears and laugh sadly at what you see, you realize that this happened because you lost your confidence and power.

Because you tumbled down the rabbit hole of someone else's vision, you are now looking for every foot and toe hold there is as you climb up towards the light. The one thing I will ask you to be conscious of is getting into anything and everything to make back the money you have lost. All money isn't good money and you can regain your lost confidence and power in this area without compromising your health and sanity.

You've lost valuable TIME! Now, this is one that you can't do anything about losing. Time is the one thing that we all have the same amount of, yet use very differently. All you can do here is make the best use of the time that you have ahead of you.

You've lost FAMILY! For many reading this, the person they are dealing with is a family member. As tragic as that is, know that all family isn't family. Yes, everyone has their quirks, yet you must know when to let toxic people go, even if they are family! Now, if a family member was that person you lost from your inner circle, then that HURTS...more than you may care to admit or choose to ponder.

You've lost your JOB or your BUSINESS! This isn't another one that is not easily fixable because you may not be able to get your old job back nor get your business back up and going so you can regain your clientele. Losing your confidence and power in this area has probably sent the wrong type of message and now you're fighting and scrambling to get anything close to what you were doing.

You may have not lost the knowledge, yet you've lost the platform in which to show that knowledge. And, if you ARE able to regain either one, know that you will have to do a lot of damage control because a lot of people who depended on you now doubt that you will get back to the person you were before you lost your confidence and power. This will be a frustrating process as you will be working to recoup everything we've talked about so far.

You've lost your love for your TALENTS! Remember how we talked about how you started downplaying your talents? Well, now, you find yourself in a space where you're wondering why you stopped doing those things in relation to what was spoken over you. You decided to take a moment and do it to see if you still had it...and you do! So, you keep going and hours pass without you realizing it. You look around at what you've done and wonder what to do with it now...MAKE SOME MONEY FROM IT!

You've lost your desire to learn something new and became a ONE HIT WONDER, which you were NEVER meant to be. You let them pigeonhole you into one thing, causing you to forget all the goals, dreams, and aspirations you had.

That one who came to you didn't want you to reach your full potential, so they convinced you that going after something other than what they thought you should be doing would lead to failure.

You've started saying you're GOOD—LIES! The fact that this happened to you feels like someone pushing a needle into your eye while your hands are tied behind your back. If you see someone else living their best life, that irks the living FIRE out of you because you wonder why they weren't as affected by this person as you were.

I'm going to leave you alone to gather your thoughts. I have prompts in the journal for each of these that I want you to work through... See you in the next chapter.

CONFRONTATION: I HAVE TO GET MY CONFIDENCE AND POWER BACK!

Becoming Sassily You means regaining your lost confidence and power, which starts with YOU! It's time out for reminiscing over what was done to you or said to you, it's time to get YOU back! That has nothing to do with anyone else.

One of the first things you need to do is give yourself some GRACE because this is going to take time to fix. There is no quick fix for regaining lost confidence and power. While you may dwell on how far you've fallen, you aren't meant to stay there! If you do, you will never get back to the person you were and are meant to be.

Since we've already spoken about what you've lost, the next step in giving yourself grace is to become solution-oriented. You must get your heart and mind back right so that you can focus on the hard reset you will have to endure.

I'm going to put these in the journal, but I want to talk about them here.

In becoming solution-oriented, you will have to rebuild your inner circle and this will hurt some because you will encounter some hurt feelings if you are working to bring someone back into your life.

Rebuilding your inner circle requires you to answer seven VERY important questions:

1. Who do I need to contact to help me regain my confidence and power?

2. What are the actions that I need to take to regain my confidence and power?

3. When do I want to get started with what I need to do to regain my confidence and power?

4. Where do I need to go to do the work I need to do to regain my confidence and power?

5. Why do I need to regain my confidence and power? What will happen if I stay the way I am now?

6. How am I going to do the work I need to do to regain my confidence and power?

7. How much time, money, and effort will it take for me to regain my confidence and power?

Now, you may look at some of these and think them unnecessary, so allow me to enlighten you on why each one of these is crucial in your pursuit to regain your lost confidence and power.

You will need to rebuild your inner circle with people who inspire, encourage, uplift, and equip you to get back to who you were and to be better once you reach that point. From there, you need people around you who will push, challenge, stretch, press, and annoy you to greatness all while giving you the tough love that you need for you to stay on track. You've already dealt with someone who wanted you to whine and wallow in misery, so it's time out for that.

You need to define your actions steps so that you can get back to who you were and move forward from there. You know what it took for you to lose your confidence and power, so now you need to focus on crafting a plan of action to get them back. This will be an uncomfortable list to make, but you must confront who you need to help you as well as what it's going to take to get things done.

You need to put deadlines on yourself because time breeds excuses, which you no longer have the luxury of making because you can't afford to lose anything else! ENOUGH IS ENOUGH! Treat each action step like an appointment. Enter it into your phone and give it every reminder alert your phone will allow you to have. Tell your inner circle what they are so that they can not only help if it's in their zone of genius to do so, but also to hold you accountable.

You need to know if you need to leave

your home, city, state, or even country to get what you need! You may not want to, but it's no longer about anything other than you getting what you need. Even in a digital world in trying times, there are some things you will have to leave your four walls and familiar circumstance to get done.

Your why is the most important question of all seven. If you don't understand that your life will be worse if you refuse to deal with this and get you back, then you will stay right where the person who planted you buried you! Also, know that your bounce back isn't for or about making anybody else proud but YOURSELF! I tell people that all the time! Don't worry about who else will be proud of you once you regain your confidence and power...this is about YOU!

You need to know how to go about the action steps that you have. This is your step by step process of performing those actions. Find out what the steps are, make a list of the things that you need, get those things, lay them all out, and then get to work!

Anything worth regaining is going to take time, money, and effort—regaining lost confidence and power is NOT free by ANY means! While you may be hoping that you catch a deal on a person, place, thing, or idea, you have to come to grips with the fact that may not happen, but don't use that as an excuse to not do something. There is more than one way to do things, even if you have to trade, barter, or work it off—if it's not life-threatening, illegal, or immoral, then it's time to get it done.

I'm going to leave you to the journal for

the rest. I don't want to spoil the exercises
too much!

COMMITMENT: I WILL NEVER LOSE MY CONFIDENCE AND POWER AGAIN!

The final part of Becoming Sassily You is setting the rules and boundaries for your life so that you TEACH people HOW to treat you! What you allow will most assuredly continue! I'm going to pull in a few of my 12 Rules of Being Dynamically Different to help you here:

1. **Stop letting people pick your brain**—this is all about increasing your discernment and speaking up

when something doesn't look, sound, or smell right. This is also about knowing when to draw the line, and not only in business, but in life as well. Someone picking your brain is how you lost your confidence and power in the first place! Don't let anyone rent space in your head like that EVER again.

2. **Set boundaries**—people need to know YOUR who, what, when, where, why, how, and how much...and you need to STICK TO IT! I don't care WHO it is! NEVER let someone cross the line you draw in the same with giving them a reason to regret doing so. If you do, you will find yourself right back on that hamster wheel, hoping that it will be different this time around.

3. **Stop helping others at the expense of YOUR goals and dreams**—part of losing your confidence and power is being pulled into someone else's who knows that you have things to do. We talked about this in an earlier chapter. Make yourself a priority. Start and end your day with YOU and what YOU need to do. Let your yes be yes, your no be no, and your word be your bond without feeling guilty for sticking to your standards. That same person you sacrifice yourself to help will turn right around and disrespectfully ask you why you are still working on something you should have already been done with!

4. **Unleash and heal your inner little kid**—one of the things that you'll have to do to keep your confidence

and power is to bring those childhood favorite things to do back into your life. For example, I LOVE doing color by number activities and even have a coloring app on my phone for it! It's a stress reliever for me. I even still have some of my favorite books from my childhood... What can you bring back after you make peace with that little one?

5. **Don't waste time focusing on where you aren't and can't be back at right now and work toward what you CAN get to at this moment**—as hard as that is, you must learn to celebrate the small wins and take the baby steps that are necessary at this stage in your recovery of the person you once were. When you make the smallest good thing insignificant or

allow someone else to do so, you are sending yourself into a dangerous downward and backward spiral that you don't need to be in at all. Focus on your forward! That's why you set goals and action steps toward said goals.

6. **Don't become numbers focused when it comes to your inner circle or needs that arise**—if you only have one person in your corner, take on the world with them even if you have to do so with a water gun and a plastic spoon! If you must prioritize things and focus on the lowest cost thing first, do that and plan for the rest to get done according to the goals and deadlines that you set.

7. **Don't be stalled by someone else's procrastination**—if they are a part

of your journey, but not ready to play their part, find someone else to do it and keep it moving! You don't have time to waste and you will soon see that, had you waited for that person, you would have become stuck, stale, stagnant, and sunken. Let them know what you need, how you need it, and when and move accordingly.

8. **Commit to only deal with people who respect your time and effort—** anyone else is officially a NON-FACTOR! Allowing disrespect for your time and effort is another way you lost your confidence and power, so we can't allow that to happen anymore. If the boundaries that you set, the time you gave, and the effort you have given are not reciprocated when it SHOULD BE, then you know

that this is someone whom you need to stay away from in the future. If the person you encounter is someone you've already had this issue with, then RUN and don't look back!

9. **Don't wait on anyone else to move before you move on to your next thing**—you don't have TIME to wait for anyone on your journey. If both of you are working on regaining your lost confidence and power, yet they are dragging their feet, then LEAVE THEM!

These may seem harsh, yet they are all necessary because you don't go back to the place you were unfairly pulled into in the first place. Incorporating these rules into your personal and professional life will help you to see through people's mess real quick and help you weed out those who seek to take your confidence and power from you.

Get all those daggon dark colors out of your closet!

Keep refining and perfecting those talents!

Laugh in the face of anyone who tries to tell you that you are less than what you are!

Tell yourself why they're WRONG about you!

Now that you've made it this far, I can only hope and pray that you keep going from here. If you feel like you're stuck or need that extra nudge, please don't hesitate to reach out to me!

ABOUT THE AUTHOR

Tammie T. Polk is a Goal and Dream Fulfillment Coach for the married, Christian professional woman with kids who battles with doing what she wants to do because of the demands placed on her life.

As the CEO and Owner of Professionally Sassy, LLC, her goal and joy is lovingly annoying women to greatness by helping them to eliminate excuses and excel in life and business and take a break from reality when needed.

Since September 2015, she has penned, lent her voice or words to, and published over 80 books on life, faith, family, ministry, education, business, and fiction.

When she's not terrorizing her readers by releasing a book every 30 days or so, you can find her lovingly annoying her husband and three daughters while enjoying her hometown of Memphis, TN.

You can reach Tammie with any questions about this or any of her other books, her coaching programs, or to book her for your next event by using either of the following outlets:

- Facebook: Professionally Sassy, LLC
- Instagram: Professionally Sassy
- Twitter: ProfessionSassy
- Website: professionallysassy.me
- Phone: 877-287-1197
- E-mail: tammie@professionallysassy.me

www.ingramcontent.com/pod-product-compliance
Lightning Source LLC
Chambersburg PA
CBHW051417250726
48655CB00003B/1091